PET OWNER'S GUIDE TO THE
LEOPARD GECKO

Noel and Janet Morgan

RINGPRESS

ABOUT THE AUTHORS

Noel and Janet Morgan have been active in the exotic animal world for more than 15 years, and have studied and bred a huge variety of animal species, including invertebrates, reptiles and amphibians, among them the Leopard Gecko. They were the first in the UK to open a privately-run reptile zoo, which started in 1990 on the Gower Coast. Since then, Noel and Janet have owned and run specialist pet shops, offering help and advice to new keepers of exotic pets.

Janet is now a full-time lecturer and assessor in Animal Care at a local college. While Noel lectures occasionally, he concentrates more on writing, drawing on his experiences of working with a diversity of animals from primates to spiders.

PHOTOGRAPHY
Fred Holmes.

Published by Ringpress Books,
A Division of INTERPET LTD
Vincent Lane, Dorking, Surrey RH4 3YX

First published 2002
©2002 Ringpress Books Limited. All rights reserved

Design: Rob Benson

ISBN 1 86054 124 0

Printed and bound in Hong Kong through Printworks International Ltd.

CONTENTS

5

BREEDING AND REARING 44

Sexing; Climate;
Courtship; Nest boxes;
Egg-laying; Incubators;
Heaters; Incubation;
Sex influence;
Hatching; Rearing.

6

THE GECKO VARIETIES 55

The four sub-families (Gekkoninae; Eublepharine,
Diplodactylinae; Spherodactylinae): The Tokay Gecko;
The Wonder Gecko; House Geckos; Bibrons Gecko;
Moorish Geckos or Wall Geckos; Madagascar Day Geckos.

7

HEALTH CARE AND AILMENTS 70

Common ailments (Cuts and
grazes; Skin shedding; Tail
shedding; Mouth rot);
Parasites; External parasites
(Ticks, Mites); Internal
parasites; Non-feeding; Colds.

1 Introducing The Leopard Gecko

The Leopard Gecko *(Eublepharus macularius)* must rank as one of the most endearing lizards on the planet. It grows to a modest 25 to 35 cm (10 to 14 inches) in length and has a temperament which is usually more placid than most household puppies. Is it any wonder that these creatures are so popular among reptile-keepers?

ORIGIN

Leopard Geckos come from the countries of the Middle East, and north from Iran to Pakistan, inhabiting rocky outcrops in deserts and in mountainous regions.

APPEARANCE

An adult Leopard Gecko is covered in spots with light

The Leopard Gecko is a member of the lizard family, and has a pleasing temperament.

brown, black and yellow markings, and large tuberculate scales, which give the lizard a 'warty' appearance, although it is actually dry and soft to the touch.

The tail is particularly fat, almost turnip-like, while the eyes, with their pronounced eyelids, look as if they belong on a cartoon character of a Hollywood starlet.

Being easy to keep, and able to breed readily in captivity, the Leopard Gecko is the ideal candidate for any first-time lizard-keeper, though most experienced reptile-keepers, even ones with large collections, still boast a colony of Leopard Geckos somewhere among their menagerie.

REPTILE PETS

Reptiles have been kept as pets for many years, but it is really only over the last decade or so that the hobby has progressed.

Years ago, reptile ownership tended to be restricted to fairly isolated individuals who kept one or two species. Now there are also groups of people keeping massive collections, and some of them are involved with major breeding projects – either for profit or, indeed, just to be able to say "we did it!"

As the hobby has grown in strength, the old image of reptile-keepers being a strange race of people has faded. Reptile-keeping is now an acknowledged pastime, enjoyed by a cross-section of society.

SUITABILITY?

If you are considering joining the happy throng of reptile-keepers, you must first ask yourself some pertinent questions.

The Leopard Gecko is relatively easy to care for, and makes an ideal choice for the novice reptile-keeper.

It is important to understand what is involved in keeping a reptile as a pet.

- Do I want a pet that I can handle and play with?
- Do I want a pet to show off to my friends?
- Will Granny have a fit if she comes to visit and sees my pet running around the living room?
- Do I want a pet as a status symbol, so that I can stand out in a crowd?

If you answer yes to any of the above questions then, please, reconsider your choice of pet; surely a dog or a budgie would fit the bill far better.

On the other hand, if you want not just a pet but a hobby, with all the rewards of maintaining not just an animal but its whole environment, then reptiles could be for you.

RESPONSIBILITY

To be a responsible hobbyist, you do not just have to maintain the animals in your charge, although this is obviously paramount. You also need to promote the true nature of reptiles.

The vast majority of reptiles held in captivity pose absolutely no threat to the wellbeing of the human race whatsoever.

There are, admittedly, some species of reptiles that are quite capable of causing serious injury, or indeed fatalities, but these are very much in the minority. Such animals are rarely found in captive collections.

Most countries have sensible legislation which prohibits the keeping of any animal considered potentially dangerous unless licensed by an appropriate authority.

Private animal-keepers can only obtain such a licence once they have satisfied the appropriate authority that all the necessary requirements for keeping such animals are fully met.

Why private reptile-keepers should want to keep potentially dangerous creatures in their homes is a bit of a mystery.

There is a plethora of reptiles suitable for hobbyists that are completely harmless, ranging from the delightful Leopard Gecko to many medium-sized snakes, such as corn snakes, whose placid temperament could shame your average bunny rabbit.

ATTITUDE
The common public perception of reptiles, which is surely due only to ignorance, tends to be that these are dangerous, poisonous, slimy animals whose sole aim in life is to eat people or, at the very

The Leopard Gecko will give you a fascinating insight into lizard behaviour.

Close observation means that you will be able to spot signs of trouble at an early stage.

least, to take up residence in either human shoes or beds.

This erroneous view is, all too often, perpetuated by a small group of hobbyists, what could be described as the 'macho brigade'. These are people who are attracted to animals for all the wrong reasons.

Instead of keeping reptiles as a hobby, in order to observe and to learn about a fascinating branch of the animal kingdom, their energies seem to be devoted to purchasing something which has the potential to scare other people.

They have no regard for, and have done no prior research into, the animal's needs and requirements.

Their choice of 'pet' is usually a reptile that is large and ferocious-looking. Presumably, in their eyes, handling such an animal demonstrates to the world just how strong and courageous they are.

They delight in the chaos they

can cause by walking into their local pub with a large python wrapped around their neck, without a thought for any unfortunate patrons with a real phobia about snakes.

REWARDS

Although there are many reptiles suitable for the beginner or novice keeper, this book concentrates on the Leopard Gecko, renowned as one of the easiest reptiles to keep in captivity. By the time you have finished reading this book, you will have all the information you need to successfully maintain, and even breed, Leopard Geckos, but never be afraid to experiment.

The best judge of an animal's wellbeing should be the person who is in daily contact with it.

- Only you can pick up on your individual pet's habits or even idiosyncrasies.
- It is you who should spot any anomalies in your pet's behaviour long before the physical signs of any problem become apparent.
- As with fish-keeping, the majority of problems can be easily remedied as long as they are recognised early enough.

So, welcome to the hobby. May you find the following pages of use and get as much pleasure out of keeping reptiles as we have.

2 The Right Choice

It is essential, when considering buying a gecko, to go for the captive-bred animals rather than the wild-caught market.

Many species of geckos are relatively easy to breed in captivity and, indeed, are bred in large numbers both by individual private keepers and by large commercial dealers supplying direct to the pet trade.

Captive-bred animals should, generally, have had little or no contact with either disease or parasites and, if reared properly, should be resilient against any such infections should mishaps or bad husbandry occur.

Generally, wild-caught geckos are marginally cheaper than captive-bred specimens, but this is a false economy. It only takes one vet's bill to swallow up any saving

Make sure the geckos you buy have been bred and reared in captivity.

Captive-bred reptiles will usually be stronger and healthier than wild-caught ones.

you might enjoy. It is strongly recommended that any novice chooses captive-bred every time, thus avoiding most potential problems at the outset.

BREED PROTECTION

Wild-caught reptiles are generally captured en masse, then held in conditions that can, at best, be described as overcrowded and Spartan, before being shipped, somewhat unceremoniously, to a wholesaler in any one of a number of different countries.

These animals which, by this time, are suffering from severe stress and dehydration, and are also probably infested with parasites, are then placed in unclean vivaria which recently housed other wild-caught reptiles suffering from similar ailments.

These vivaria, contaminated by the pathogens left behind by the previous occupants, then pass on their unwelcome inhabitants to the unfortunate, already weakened, newcomers. By the time the poor wretches have reached your local pet shop they are quite often about to knock heavily on heaven's door.

If you are new to reptile-keeping, do you really want to start with all these possible problems that could so easily be avoided? Also, by buying a wild-caught animal, you are encouraging a very undesirable trade.

Many animals are becoming endangered world-wide. This happens not just because of man's penchant for clearing vast acres of all that messy vegetation and replacing them with clean-cut, concrete edifices and roads, but also through the over-collection of wild animals for the pet trade.

With the number of geckos produced in captivity, how can we really justify continuing the trade in geckos taken from the wild?

BUYER BEWARE

Whether you decide to purchase your gecko from a pet shop or a private breeder, there are a few things that you should always look out for.

Check with the vendor whether the animal is captive-bred or not. However, be warned. Not all pet shop owners are scrupulously honest. If possible, ask if you can be shown the animal's parents.

Look carefully at the animal's environment.

- Is it clean?
- Is there clean water?
- Is the vivarium heated?
- Does the vendor seem knowledgeable about the lizards?

If you have any doubts about the way the animal is being kept, then go elsewhere. Why put your hard-earned cash into the pocket of a dodgy dealer when there are so many decent suppliers around?

In my early days of reptile-keeping, I frequently bought animals that were being kept in somewhat unsavoury conditions just to get them out of there.

Unfortunately, my gallant actions merely resulted in me being the proud owner of an empty wallet, up to my neck in sick and ailing

If you handle a gecko, you will get an idea of its temperament.

The eyes should be bright and fully open.

animals, while the dealer, enjoying rocketing profits, went straight out and replaced everything I had bought, and more.

GET TACTILE
Make sure, before any money changes hands, that you can hold the animal. Although the majority of geckos are docile, just occasionally you can come across an individual whose temperament is not unlike that of a hormonal teenager who has just been told to turn his stereo off and go and mow the lawn!

Lizards with this sort of temperament can make better breeding stock but, unless you have masochistic tendencies, a docile specimen makes for a much better pet.

While holding the animal, you should check over its general condition. It should feel fairly chunky and robust.

TELLING TAILS
The tail should always be particularly plump and fleshy to the touch. The tail on a Leopard Gecko, for example, can be compared to a camel's hump. It acts as a sort of reservoir of fats for the animal to draw off in times of need, so it is also a good indicator of the animal's overall condition and, indeed, of how well it has been looked after.

CHECK THE EYES
Look also at the lizard's eyes. They should be fully open, bright and glossy in appearance. Geckos

with sunken, half-closed, lack-lustre eyes should be avoided, as these can be indicative of several serious health problems. It should also look alert, even curious, and wander around your hand, occasionally flicking its tongue out to taste its surroundings.

COUNT THE TOES

Another useful tip is to count its toes. There should be five on each foot on a Leopard Gecko. This does vary with different species, but a lizard can easily lose digits during shedding (see Chapter Seven). Missing digits do not appear to make any major difference to the animal's quality of life, but may well act as a starting point for a possible discount on the price of the lizard. You also need to check the skin and the condition of the toes.

Check the feet to make sure there are no missing digits.

APPETITE

It is also a good idea to ask to see the animal being fed before you buy it.

It is not necessarily a bad omen if it refuses food in front of you; after all, it may have eaten just before you got there, or even be nervous of being watched while eating.

If, on the other hand, the animal does feed in front of you, then you will have another indication about its general health.

NUMBERS

Like the vast majority of reptiles, geckos can be kept quite happily on their own. But, if you consider that the cost of all the equipment for housing one lizard is basically the same as housing two or more, depending on the size of your vivarium, then surely it makes sense to keep a small group. The only extra cost incurred will be for feeding, which, when compared to the cost of feeding a cat or dog, is quite nominal. Should you start with a single Leopard Gecko though, you could always add more at a later date.

GROUPS

Many species such as the Leopard, Tokay, Bibrons, Turkish,

A good appetite is a reliable indication that the gecko is in reasonable health.

Phelsumas and others, can be kept in groups, usually with one dominant adult male.

The danger comes when, or if, you attempt to mix species. You will need to research carefully each intended resident before mixing them in the same vivarium. Animals that can be kept in groups are not necessarily social species and may attack other species on sight.

Sad to say, a number of pet shops actually mix various lizards from different continents, and totally different habitats, in the same vivarium in order, apparently, to save space.

Needless to say, this policy has disastrous results. Certain species will attack and kill any other species that enters its territory. Others, such as the Tokay, are large enough to eat young House Geckos without much consideration.

BALANCING ACT

When it comes to balancing populations, especially in respect of the Leopard Gecko, then one of the most important factors to consider is the mixing of the sexes.

Female Leopard Geckos can be housed together in any quantities, and, although they will often develop their own pecking order, any real squabbling among them is unusual.

Males, on the other hand, are

a great deal more territorial. You can usually keep two males together in the same enclosure without too many problems but, if you introduce a female to them, then fighting will almost certainly occur.

This territorial behaviour also extends to lizards of other species. Mixing Leopard Geckos with other lizards is best avoided.

Never be fooled by a Leopard Gecko's gentle and placid behaviour towards human beings. A Leopard Gecko with a grudge against a rival can be a terrifying sight, and the ensuing battle often results in severe injuries and even fatalities.

Mixing the sizes of Leopard Geckos is also to be avoided, as a large adult could easily consider a hatchling as a potential snack.

Similarly, an adult Leopard Gecko might not dream of harming a youngster sharing the same vivarium, but the youngster might spend his days in abject terror at the prospect of being eaten. As you can imagine, living under such stress can lead to an awfully short life.

SEXES

Sexing immature Leopard Geckos is, unfortunately, nigh on impossible, so, if you start with youngsters, it really is a matter of

There are a number of gecko species that will live happily in groups.

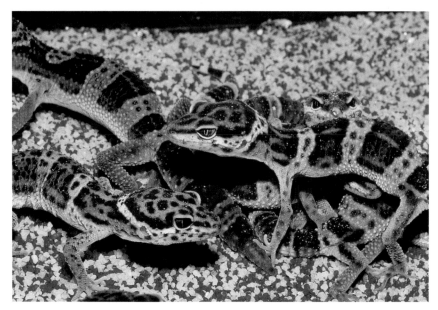

The skin of hatchling Leopard Geckos is banded.

pot luck to get the sexing right.

You can, however, make an educated guess (See Chapter Five: Breeding and Rearing). If you do get the sexing wrong, do not panic. Any really aggressive behaviour should not become evident until the animals reach sexual maturity, which is seldom within the first twelve months.

Prior to sexual maturity, the physical differences between the sexes become quite clear. Separating any unwanted males or females from the group can usually be done long before any real problems occur.

Unwanted or surplus Leopard Geckos can usually be sold to, or exchanged with, most dealers involved with reptiles.

AGES

Whether you decide to buy hatchling or adult geckos is, really, just a matter of personal preference. If one of your main considerations is breeding, then, obviously, you would look for either adult or sub-adult specimens. If, on the other hand, you would prefer to keep your lizards just as pets, then hatchlings would probably suit you better.

Recently-hatched geckos can be easily recognised because they have a small line, a shaped mark, on the abdomen. This is where the umbilical cord was attached to the lizard in the egg. This scar usually heals up within the first few months.

Hatchling Leopard Geckos are also banded, not spotted. The bands break up into spots, gradually, each time the lizard sheds its skin. It seldom takes on its adult colours until it is several months old.

HEALTHY GROWTH

Unlike mammals, most reptiles carry on growing till the day they die, with the fastest growth occurring in the first six to twelve months, slowing considerably as the animal gets older. The growth rate of a Leopard Gecko is determined by several factors. Generally, lizards kept under optimum conditions with a good feeding regime will grow considerably faster than a lizard kept within its basic requirements.

There can, however, be exceptions to the rule. Occasionally you will see some individuals kept on meagre rations in the most humble vivarium grow like athletes on steroids, while their siblings, housed in a palatial vivarium with regular meals, seem to hardly grow at all.

Adult Leopard Geckos can easily exceed 30 cm (12 inches) in length but, with a lifespan often recorded at over 30 years, the danger of purchasing an individual who has been pensioned off and waiting for the call to the great vivarium in the sky is fairly remote.

3 Setting Up Home

Acontainer full of fish, for viewing or for propagation, is called an aquarium; a container full of reptiles, for viewing or propagation, is called a vivarium.

VIVARIA
The vivarium does not need to be anything fancy; old fish tanks make excellent vivaria, or you can easily make your own one out of wood. There are many reliable, ready-made vivaria on the market but you can always take the DIY route. The important requirements for a vivarium are security, ventilation and hygiene.

You do not need to be a master

The most important considerations for a vivarium are security, ventilation and hygiene.

craftsman to make your own vivarium because, at the end of the day, it is little more than a box fitted with a door and a window.

MATERIALS

Use a material that can easily be wiped or scrubbed. Laminated chipboard is one of the most favoured materials, though well-varnished pine or plywood is equally suitable. Simply cut two pieces of wood to identical lengths. These will be for the floor and the roof. Then cut two smaller pieces for the sides. These will give you the basic box shape.

For the back of the vivarium you can either use the same material, or tack on a piece of hardboard, with the shiny side facing inwards for ease of cleaning. This cuts down the weight and also the cost.

On the front of the vivarium, attach a plinth to the floor, which stops the substrate from spilling out every time you open the door. The plinth can be made from a piece of timber roughly 10 cm (4 inches) high, fitted flush to the edge of the floor and sides.

SIZE

Vivarium size is probably one of the most contentious points among reptile-keepers.

Leopard Geckos in the wild are

Plan the vivarium so that it is easy to clean.

Leopard Geckos are not great climbers, so the height of the vivarium is not of major importance.

not particularly gregarious, so is it fair to cram several adults into a small vivarium? There are several, very successful, mass breeders of Leopard Geckos who operate an almost battery-farm system for lizards, arguing that if the animals were not happy then they would not be such prolific breeders.

This is a fair point, but the concept that the quality of life, and the longevity, of such animals compares favourably with those kept in less cramped conditions can certainly be challenged.

Although hatchling Leopard Geckos, for the first few months of their lives, can be kept quite happily in the small plastic tanks with clip-on lids that most of the major pet manufacturers produce, Leopard Geckos reaching sexual maturity should be given reasonable room.

It is recommended that a vivarium for a group of one male and one or two females of breeding size should measure at least 60 cm (24 inches) wide by 40 cm (16 inches) tall by 40 cm (16 inches) deep. For every addition to the vivarium, you should add a further 15 cm (6 inches) width and depth.

Extra height is not particularly important; Leopard Geckos will often climb logs and plants while out for a nightly constitutional, but tend to leave most arboreal antics to the birds and monkeys.

DOORS

On top of the plinth you attach some sliding door runners, which can be obtained from most DIY stores. Fit the thinner strip on to the plinth. Fit the thicker strip flush to the edge inside the roof.

You then need two pieces of glass, cut roughly 5 mm (0.2 inches) taller than the gap between the top of the bottom runner and the bottom of the top runner, so that the glass can be pushed upwards into the top runner, then dropped into the groove of the bottom runner.

The width of each piece of glass should be at least 2 cm (0.8 inches) wider than half the width of the vivarium so that, with the doors closed, you have an overlap of at least 4 cm (1.6 inches).

If, like me, your glass cutting skills leave a lot to be desired, do not worry. Most glass suppliers readily cut glass to size.

VENTILATION

Ventilation in a vivarium is a must, and can be achieved quite easily and cheaply.

Kitchen cupboard vents are

Try to keep one area of the vivarium slightly moist.

Reptiles cannot control their own body temperature, so providing the correct heating is a crucial factor.

good ones to use. These usually consist of a plate with either small holes or slots cut out of them. Cut, or drill, a suitably sized opening in either the back or side of the vivarium, and then use the plate to cover the gap.

This allows fresh air into the vivarium without letting the lizards, or their food, escape.

Without ventilation, there is the danger of condensation building up, leading to high humidity and a subsequent myriad of problems with bacterial and fungal infections for the inhabitants.

A relative humidity of between 20 and 30 per cent is ideal for Leopard Geckos and can easily be maintained by keeping a small corner of the vivarium slightly moist.

It is a good idea to have a small handful of sphagnum moss in one corner of the vivarium and to spray it with water regularly.

HEATING

Probably the most critical factor in keeping any exotic reptile is temperature. The obvious question is, what is the best temperature? The optimum temperature is around 25 degrees C to 29 degrees C (84 degrees F), dropping a few degrees at night,

A sand substrate can result in injury.

Bark chippings provide a natural-looking surface.

but it is doubtful that a constant temperature of 29 degrees C (84 degrees F) would be maintained in the wild.

Reptiles are unable to generate or regulate their own body temperature, unlike mammals that can shiver when they are cold, or pant and perspire when they are too warm.

Reptiles have to make do with basking under the sun when too cold and hiding in the shade when too hot. The best way to allow any captive reptile to follow this natural behaviour is to create a thermal gradient within the vivarium.

This is very easily achieved by merely placing whatever heat source you have decided upon close to one end of the vivarium. This way it does not matter too much (within reason) if the hot end is too hot and the cold end too cold.

By always offering the animals a choice of temperature, they can decide what is best for them.

Care should always be taken that the animals cannot get into direct contact with any heat source capable of causing burns.

Reptiles do not seem to recognise the sensation of burning and frequently have been seen to bask so close to the heat source that they end up with horrendous blisters.

There are several ways of attaining the correct temperature. Heater mats, thin plastic mats containing an electrical element, are probably one of the most commonly used methods.

A heater mat, used in conjunction with an appropriate-strength light bulb, provides both extra heat and light during daylight hours, and, with the bulb turned off at night, allows a reduction in temperature, simulating the temperature fluctuations found in the Leopard Gecko's natural environment.

LIGHTING

Leopard Geckos are nocturnal, so any lighting that you fit is really for your benefit only. Red light seems not to register with reptiles, so fitting a red light bulb to the vivarium enables you to watch the lizards, while they consider it dark enough to be out and about.

SUBSTRATES

When deciding what to use on the floor of a vivarium, most people understandably opt for sand. Unfortunately, most of the sand available is totally unsuitable. Common builder's sand, for example, contains very sharp granules of silicone which, if ingested, can actually scratch the lining of the stomach, possibly leading to peritonitis. This can easily happen to an over-zealous Leopard Gecko launching itself headlong at an unsuspecting cricket.

Another problem associated with the ingestion of sand is impaction. This occurs when particles of indigestible material such as sand, collect and block either the digestive or excretory tract, often with fatal results.

There are many alternatives to sand. There is, of course, the old faithful – newspaper. Old

Geckos like places to hide, and this should be considered when planning your decor.

newspapers are cheap and clean.

Woodshavings or woodchip (not sawdust) make another good substrate, being inexpensive and easily obtainable. The ornamental bark chippings found in some garden centres can look very decorative, but the uncleaned variety has been known to harbour parasites. This can be overcome by placing the bark chips in the microwave for a minute or two.

Peat moss, as long as it is not too damp, is another alternative, but does not look quite right for a desert set-up. A favourite substrate for Leopard Geckos is corncob granules which look, at first glance, similar to sand but are slightly paler. The main drawback to corncob granules is that they are comparatively expensive and not as readily available as some of the alternatives mentioned.

DECORATION

How you decorate the vivarium is largely down to personal taste, but keep one major factor in mind. Leopard Geckos, in common with most reptiles, are inherently shy and must be offered plenty of cover and hiding places in order to thrive. There are many ways of achieving this.

Probably the most effective is adding foliage to the vivarium, and plastic plants are a lot easier to clean and last a lot longer than real plants. Adding caves is another good idea. These can be made of rocks (carefully secured lest you end up owning a pancake gecko) or wood.

There are many ready-made hidey-holes for reptiles on the market but you can use materials that Mother Nature so kindly leaves free all around us.

Driftwood is probably the best wood to use, partly because of the interesting shapes you so often come across and partly because the sea has done most of the cleaning work for you, but most rocks and branches are fine to use once cleaned.

One of best methods of ensuring that the items you are placing in the vivarium are safe is thorough, vigorous scrubbing with a wire brush, or a suitable alternative.

Follow this up by pouring several panfuls of boiling water over them. This will, in effect, sterilise them.

4 Caring For Your Gecko

In general, Leopard Geckos have a very placid temperament and can easily be picked up. To do this, gently place the flat of your hand in front of your gecko and then encourage it to walk on to your hand by gently prodding it from behind. This applies to most docile species of gecko.

HANDLING

Once on your hand, you can allow your gecko to explore you. The gecko will often climb up your arm and on to your shoulder where it will almost take up residence. Be warned, though, there is always the danger of forgetting the gecko is there and then wandering off down to the local shops!

Seriously though, even the most tame and well-handled Leopard Geckos can sometimes get it into their heads to attempt the hundred-yard dash for no apparent reason. A fall on to a cushion or a

A tame gecko will not object to being handled.

thick carpet, though best avoided, seldom causes serious injury, but a fall on to a hard surface can lead to a sombre funeral service in the back garden.

NERVOUS REPTILES

Picking up a more nervous specimen must be done with some care. However, a bite from a Leopard Gecko is, at worst, unpleasant and cannot compare with the sort of injury that can be

33

If your gecko is used to the routine of being handled, he will become quite relaxed.

inflicted by an unhappy hamster or a grumbling gerbil. Should you be unfortunate enough to have a Leopard Gecko clamp on to your finger, the best course of action is to smile sweetly and wait until it lets go. The feeling is no worse than a tight pinch.

If you try and forcibly remove the animal, then the chances are that it will try to hold on tighter and, although the teeth are small, they are very sharp and slightly curved and, consequently, quite able to tear your skin.

If this happens, the usual rules apply as for any minor cut or graze: wash the wound and apply a small dab of antiseptic ointment. This is not to overstate the damage a Leopard Gecko can inflict but, hopefully, by letting you know what to expect, you can

avoid the natural reaction of throwing your hand up in surprise and accidentally flinging the poor beast into the nearest wall.

The correct way to pick up a nervous gecko that may bite would be to use gloves and grasp it gently but confidently around the neck with your thumb and forefinger, using the remaining fingers to support its body.

Great care must be taken *never* to handle a Leopard Gecko roughly, as their skin is quite delicate and can easily tear. Should this happen, seek veterinary assistance, as such a wound could easily become infected.

THE TAIL

When trying to catch a timid Leopard Gecko there is often a temptation to grab the lizard by

Once the tail has become detached, it can still thrash around for a few minutes, fooling the predator into thinking he has caught his 'prize'.

A new tail will grow back, but it may be slightly deformed.

nature's great handle, the tail. *Don't,* unless you want it to come off in your hand.

Leopard Geckos, like many other lizards, have a rather remarkable method of avoiding capture in the wild.

Imagine, if you will, a Leopard Gecko fleeing from the unwelcome attentions of a cat, or indeed from any other predator with a predilection for saurian stew. At some time during the chase, the first part of the lizard's anatomy to come within the predator's reach will be its tail.

Once the tail has been seized, the lizard simply lets it go. The nerves in the now-detached tail can carry on operating for several minutes, making the tail thrash around quite violently.

This fools the predator into thinking that it has won and so can settle down to feast on such a prize.

In the meantime the lizard, totally unharmed by his ordeal, has won enough time to seek sanctuary under the nearest available rock or branch.

The missing tail does eventually

regenerate but is usually slightly
deformed, never looking as good
as the original.

*Place your gecko in a secure
container when you need to clean the
vivarium.*

HUMAN HYGIENE

Always wash your hands after
handling your pet. This is not a
rule applying just to reptiles,
though some ill-informed
scaremongers would like to have
you think so. All animals can carry
disease and common sense dictates
that basic hygiene should prevail
at all times. Some callers to our
collection have been asked to wash
their hands thoroughly before
being allowed to handle the
animals!

*A complete clean-out, when the whole
vivarium needs to be emptied, only
needs to be done on a monthly or
two-monthly basis.*

CLEANING

When it comes to keeping the
vivarium clean, Leopard Geckos
must rank as one of the most
considerate of all reptiles.

They will usually designate an
area of the vivarium as a toilet. So,
all you need to do is regularly
remove the faeces and soiled
substrate from the toilet area, and
get rid of uneaten food, such as
dead locusts and crickets, from the
rest of the living quarters.

This means that complete
emptying and scrubbing of the
vivarium need only be done on a
monthly, or two-monthly basis,

*Use an unscented disinfectant to
clean the decor.*

The Leopard Gecko has a very sensitive sense of smell, and will react adversely to strong cleaning chemicals.

depending on the number of geckos you are keeping.

When you do a thorough clean-out, observe the following points:

- Put the lizards in a safe place.
- Take out the plants and the rocks and any other decor.
- Discard the old substrate.
- Wipe the whole vivarium down with either unscented disinfectant or a mild solution of bleach.

It is important to ensure that, after thoroughly disinfecting the vivarium, all traces of the disinfectant are removed before the animals are replaced.

Most reptiles have an extremely acute sense of smell due, mainly, to what is known as the Jacobson's organ, situated in the roof of the mouth.

This acts like an on-board computer. When the tongue is extended it collects air particles, which are transferred to the Jacobson's organ when the tongue is retracted. There they are analysed to such a degree that even water can be detected over quite long distances. If you appreciate this sensitivity, you can imagine that the pungent odour of any cleaning materials could cause some distress within the confines of a vivarium.

Fresh drinking water must be available at all times.

Regular cleaning of the water bowl is essential, and fresh water should always be on offer. Contaminated water is probably the quickest way to cause disease in any animal.

EATING

Leopard Geckos are totally carnivorous and, in the wild, will eat anything small enough for them to overpower, from virtually all invertebrates to even small rodents. In captivity, however, it is very difficult to offer quite such a variety. The standard foods available through the pet trade are crickets, locusts, mealworms and pinkies.

Invertebrates should be offered live, as Leopard Geckos are predatory animals, not scavengers, and tend not to recognise even the most succulent of grubs as food if it is lying, totally inanimate, on the floor of the vivarium. Some books on the subject of feeding insects, and crickets in particular, to lizards, suggest chilling the insects in a refrigerator for several minutes prior to feeding in order to slow them down, thus making them easier for the Leopard Geckos to catch.

CHASING FOOD

There are two reasons why it is preferable to see the animal working for its supper.

The first is that chasing and catching prey is probably the only form of exercise open to a lizard

Chasing food provides exercise and stimulation for the captive gecko.

that is kept in a vivarium.

The second is that being able to observe the natural and almost cat-like way in which a Leopard Gecko stalks and finally pounces on its intended meal is surely part of the reason for keeping a slice of nature in your living room.

How often, and how much, you should feed your lizards is another one of those areas very much open for debate, particularly among the lizards themselves. Reptiles in captivity are prone to obesity. In the wild, they will gorge themselves should the opportunity arise, as they can never be too certain when their next meal will present itself.

In captivity, this instinctive behaviour drives them to eat far more than they need or, indeed, far more than is good for them.

Obesity in reptiles carries the same health risks as it does for humans, including circulatory

Crickets are the staple source of diet for Leopard Geckos kept in captivity.

problems, heart disease and a shortened life span. It also decreases the chances of them breeding.

About the only time a Leopard Gecko is active is when it is hungry and hunting for food. It will, of course, forgo this exercise if the next meal is delivered before it has actually felt the need to get up and go and look for it.

FEEDING REGIMES

A favoured feeding regime is to place slightly more food into the vivarium than will be eaten in the initial frenzy, then leaving the next feed until such a time as the geckos are seen to be wandering

the vivarium, obviously peckish.

This can regularly take several days to a week. Occasional periods without food will do absolutely no harm to a Leopard Gecko and, in fact, such a regime is close to their natural feeding pattern and quite beneficial.

DIET OPTIONS

CRICKETS

This is the usual staple diet offered to Leopard Geckos. They are relatively cheap, reasonably nutritious and readily available from pet shops dealing with reptiles.

Crickets come in a variety of

Waxmoth larvae can be used to tempt a gecko's appetite.

sizes, from pinhead-size micro-crickets (usually fed to hatchling spiders and amphibians) to veritable giants (well, half a thumb-length anyway) suitable for adult Leopard Geckos.

When deciding what size cricket to feed your lizard, the general rule of thumb is to feed nothing bigger than the lizard's head, but, to be honest, a healthy Leopard Gecko should quite easily be able to subdue a cricket twice that size.

LOCUSTS

These are a bit more expensive than crickets and not quite as nutritious and should, ideally, be used more as a regular treat to break up the monotony of eating the same thing day after day rather than as a staple diet.

MEALWORMS

These are not actually worms but the larvae of the flour beetle, *Tenebrio molitor* (scourge of the bakery), and are the least nutritional of all. They have very little meat wrapped up in a relatively thick layer of chitin (skin), but they are cheap and do make an excellent stand-by food.

Mealworms will pupate into a beetle that very few lizards find palatable, but if the pupae are kept cool then metamorphosis can be delayed by several months.

A vitamin supplement is essential to ensure your gecko receives all the nutrition it requires.

WAXMOTH LARVAE

Some pet shops specialising in reptiles occasionally offer waxmoth larvae for sale. These are a small grub not unlike mealworms but with a very thin skin so they are easily digestible.

They are cultured in a very sweet medium, giving them a distinctive flavour that Leopard Geckos and, indeed, most small-to-medium size lizards find quite irresistible. In fact, waxmoths can be a fairly serious problem in beehives where they find the honey particularly appetising.

As with most popular food (think of humans and chocolate biscuits, for example), waxmoth larvae should be fed quite sparingly, mainly as a treat, but

they are particularly good for encouraging a problem-feeding lizard to eat.

PINKIES

Day-old frozen mice, known as pinkies, are an excellent food favoured by some of the larger Leopard Geckos. These should be thoroughly defrosted and, in an attempt to make them appear alive, offered by hand to the lizard.

Care should be taken that an over-enthusiastic Leopard Gecko does not mistake your finger for a pinkie, resulting in an unpleasant experience for you and a frustrating one for the animal.

The best way to defrost a pinkie is to let it stand at room temperature for about thirty minutes.

Many an impatient reptile-keeper has made the mistake of using the microwave, resulting in a mess reminiscent of an explosion in a butcher's shop.

HAPPY HUNTING

One way of introducing more variety into your lizard's diet is to collect your own insects from your garden, but do think carefully about what invertebrates you intend to catch.

Most moths, worms, grasshoppers and even spiders are quite suitable, but some caterpillars and slugs can be unpalatable, if not downright poisonous, so let your motto be "if in doubt, leave it out!".

There is also the risk, albeit a slight one, of inadvertently introducing parasites to your animals. However, when this is weighed up against the advantages of an increased menu, well, then you must decide for yourself.

SUPPLEMENTS

Whatever diet you offer your Leopard Geckos, it is essential to use a vitamin supplement to ensure that all your animals' dietary requirements are met. Vitamin supplements are inexpensive and readily available from most pet shops and veterinary surgeons, and can come in several forms.

There are liquid varieties that can simply be added to the drinking water; vitamin-enriched food that can be offered to the prey animals immediately prior to feeding them to your lizard (gut loading); or powder varieties that can be used for dusting the prey animals.

Our personal preference is

dusting, as most reptiles from arid regions such as Leopard Geckos tend to get most of the liquid they need from their food (although fresh water should always be on offer). This makes it very difficult to ascertain how much of the vitamin-enriched water they are actually drinking.

Similarly, how can you judge if the prey animals are taking up enough gut-loading preparation? By introducing freshly dusted invertebrates into the vivarium you can have a visual check that a good proportion of them are eaten before the powder has a chance to rub off.

The easiest method of dusting the food animals is to simply place a tablespoonful of powder in a plastic bag with the insects you intend to use and vigorously shake it, leaving the insects slightly dizzy but well coated and ready to use.

The effects of not using vitamin supplements are not particularly apparent in the short term. Over the long term, however, they can be quite devastating, resulting in general deformities, misshapen limbs and a skeleton so brittle that the slightest knock can result in broken bones.

Never underestimate the impor-tance of vitamin supplements.

5 *Breeding And Rearing*

Before discussing the possibility of breeding your Leopard Geckos, it is rather important to make sure that you have at least one of each sex. You might consider this an obvious statement, but actually there are several species of lizard capable of 'virgin birth' (parthenogenesis). In such species, males are rare, if present at all.

SEXING

Adult Leopard Geckos are reasonably easy to sex. Males are generally larger overall than the females; but, of course, unless you have access to a group of adults, it is very difficult to decide which is large and which is not.

The most obvious difference between the sexes is the pre-anal pores, which are actually small glands, situated in a group of enlarged scales on the underside of the lizard, just above the vent, which is the slit-like opening used for excretory and reproductive functions.

These enlarged scales, visible in both male and female Leopard Geckos, take the form of an inverted V shape. However, it is only in the male Leopard Gecko that the enlarged scales have the pre-anal pores, which look like a small black hole near the upper edge of each of the enlarged scales.

Another method of sexing Leopard Geckos, particularly useful in immature specimens yet to develop pre-anal pores, is to look for hemipenal swellings.

This method is by no means totally reliable but can be a valuable aid to an educated guess. To explain how to look for hemipenal swellings, it will be necessary to give a brief, and hopefully simplified, description of a Leopard Gecko's reproductive anatomy.

All male lizards and snakes have a 'penis', known as a hemipene,

Pre-anal pores of a male gecko.

With this thought in mind, perhaps just placing a pair of Leopard Geckos into a vivarium and then standing back, waiting for something to happen, is not particularly realistic.

The main factor that should be taken into account when breeding Leopard Geckos is climate. Although Leopard Geckos come from hot desert regions, there is still a marked seasonal difference between summer and winter.

This change cannot be compared with the winters endured by species from more temperate climates, where the temperatures drop so low that the reptiles have to hibernate in order to survive.

However, the winter is not just significantly cooler but there is also a noticeable reduction in the amount of food available. Leopard Geckos, like so many other animals, are not daft and they wait for the warmer weather, and more abundant food to arrive, before deciding to try and raise families.

This behaviour is quite easy to simulate in captivity. By reducing the temperature in the vivarium and operating a far less frequent feeding regime for a period of two to three months, you can then recreate an artificial spring, when the temperature and feeding are

each side of the vent. These hemipenes lie inside out from the vent towards the base of the tail and are everted for mating, somewhat like pulling off a tight sock.

Either organ can be used totally at the lizard's discretion. The swelling where the hemipenes are housed can be seen at the base of the tail.

CLIMATE

One favourite snippet of philosophy concerning the breeding of reptiles is:

"The good reptile-keeper should not strive to make his animals breed but keep them well enough to allow them to breed."

A change in temperature is the trigger for geckos to start breeding.

returned to normal.

With the onset of this artificial spring, providing that you have a male and at least one female Leopard Gecko of sufficient size and age, mating should begin.

COURTSHIP

Courtship among most lizards, Leopard Geckos included, is not exactly a hearts-and-flowers affair.

The male Leopard Gecko will stalk the female before clamping his jaws around the back of her neck, then, with her held in place, he will put one of his hind legs (and sometimes his tail) over her back legs in such a way that copulation can occur.

This biting of the female's neck, though it looks severe, seldom leads to any serious damage but, if the skin is broken, then keep a careful eye on the wound and treat it accordingly should infection set in.

Mating can last for several minutes and be repeated quite frequently.

The frequency of mating can be some cause for concern. If the male has a particularly high libido and does not have enough female companions among whom he can share his attentions, then there is always the danger of him 'worrying' the females.

If the females are observed to be constantly trying to escape from the male, even ignoring food if the male is in close proximity, then you should consider removing the male from the vivarium periodically, for at least a couple of days at a time.

Without respite from an over-amorous male's attentions, stress-related illnesses, or even the death of a female, are an almost certain eventuality.

NEST BOXES

Once a successful mating has taken place, it will take between 60 and 65 days before the female lays her eggs. Leopard Geckos generally lay two eggs after each mating, but young females frequently lay only one, particularly at the beginning of the season.

It is essential, long before the eggs are due to be laid, that the female has somewhere to lay them. She will look for a site that is both secure and humid in which to bury her eggs. If such a site is not provided, then the female will possibly discard her eggs in a totally unsuitable place where, if they are not discovered in time, they will spoil. Alternatively, and more importantly, she could become egg-bound.

It is very difficult to diagnose an egg-bound Leopard Gecko and any premature treatment could be as disastrous as the ailment itself.

If you suspect that your lizard is egg-bound, the safest treatment that you can perform is to bathe the animal in tepid water and gently massage the belly.

If this does not work, then more professional assistance will be required. Most experienced reptile-keepers and veterinary surgeons should be able to help.

The best thing I have found to use as a nest box is an old margarine or ice-cream container, with a hole cut into the side for the lizard to use as an entrance. The container should be filled to about 25 mm to 50 mm (one-fifth of an inch) depth with very damp (but not soaking) substrate.

The substrate most often used for the nest box is vermiculite, which is sterile, absorbent and quite inexpensive. There are other substrates that can be used, such as sphagnum moss, peat moss or even sand.

Although these materials are

Introduce a nest box well in advance so the female is happy to lay her eggs in it.

suitable for egg-laying, the eggs would be better off transferred on to vermiculite for incubation.

EGG-LAYING

Once the female has located the nest box, she will spend a fair amount of time in it. The time increases as she becomes nearer to laying her eggs. It is important not to disturb her too much at this time, as the nest box must be a place that she considers safe both for her and her eggs.

Whenever the female visits the nest box, it is quite natural for you to want to check to see if she has laid. You must try to curb this natural curiosity lest she abandons the nest box in fear of too much interference.

It is easy to tell when the female has actually laid her eggs, as her instinct to bury them drives her not only to whatever material is in the nest box, but also the substrate surrounding it.

This burying behaviour continues until there is a noticeable mound of material both in the nest box and in front of the entrance to it. One or two of my more enthusiastic females have even been known to drag small branches and plastic plants halfway around the vivarium to help cover the eggs.

During the period when you are expecting eggs, you should try to ensure that there is no surplus of live crickets wandering around the vivarium.

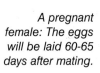

A pregnant female: The eggs will be laid 60-65 days after mating.

Crickets have a voracious appetite and will quite happily munch their way through unattended eggs. They have even been known to attack and kill lizards which, for whatever reason, are too weak to defend themselves.

INCUBATORS

An incubator is quite simply a receptacle held at a predetermined temperature. There are several good, ready-made incubators on the market but I have always gone for the cheaper option of building my own.

There are several ways of doing this. One of the more reliable methods is to utilise a small fish tank filled up to about a third with water. In the water, place an ordinary heater-thermostat, as used by tropical fish-keepers, set to the appropriate temperature.

Place the egg box on a small island so that it is just about level with the surface of the water. The humble, ordinary, house brick will suffice for this purpose.

This form of incubator is both simple and reliable, with the added bonus of keeping the humidity quite high; but do remember that most fish tank heater-thermostats must remain submerged at all times or else they will overheat and crack.

Another form of incubator, particularly useful if you are expecting to incubate several clutches of eggs at the same time, is to construct a small vivarium.

One of the main advantages of using a wooden construction, as opposed to glass, is insulation, because glass tends to lose heat quite quickly. The vivarium can then be made to the correct size for comfortably accommodating the number of eggs anticipated.

This vivarium/incubator can be fitted with one of the many excellent reptile thermostats found in good pet shops. There is a variety of suitable heaters available to connect to the thermostat, depending on what size incubator you decide to build.

It is important to ensure that, whatever form of heating you employ, the thermostat is suitable.

HEATERS

For large incubators, I tend to favour the tubular greenhouse heaters found in garden centres and specialist electrical suppliers.

One of these should be fitted to the floor of the incubator, with the eggs sited on a shelf at least several inches above.

Placing the heat source above the eggs can easily lead to them drying out, while heat sources placed under the eggs tend to warm up the damp substrate and increase the humidity. The shelf needs to be fitted with either slats or mesh to allow the heat to circulate more evenly.

Some of the other heaters available include ceramic heaters, heating cables, heated rocks and even light bulbs (though I have always found that, due to the switching action of the thermostat, light bulbs tend not to last).

For smaller incubators, a heater mat can be quite adequate but, if you are in any doubt as to the best system to use for the size of your incubator, then discuss it with your local pet shop owner. Most pet shop owners are more than happy to advise you.

Whatever form of incubator you have decided on, run it long before your eggs are due in order to ensure that the temperature has been set properly and that the incubator is holding that temperature. The best way to do this is to use a maximum/minimum thermometer. This can then tell you not only the current temperature but also what drop in temperature (if any) has occurred overnight.

Should the unexpected happen and you discover eggs before you have had a chance to build your incubator, then do not forget that old stand-by, the airing cupboard. Although not the most efficient form of incubator, the humble airing cupboard has been the beginning for many an exotic animal.

INCUBATION

Once the female has laid the eggs, they should be removed for incubation. If the substrate used in the nest box was vermiculite, then it is easier to move the box to an incubator. If not, then move the eggs to a similar container containing damp vermiculite. It really is the best medium for incubating eggs.

Great care must be taken when handling eggs. Lizard eggs are not like birds' eggs; they are soft and leathery to the touch and, if they are turned or tilted in any way, they will be ruined. If you are using your nest box, remember, of course, to seal up the entrance to the box to prevent the hatchlings from escaping.

You must also ventilate the box. If you are using a plastic tub, this

Once the female has laid her eggs, they should be removed for incubation.

is done by poking several dozen small holes in the lid with a fork.

Although, in the wild, Leopard Gecko eggs remain completely covered during incubation, in captivity it is best if you very carefully uncover about a third of each egg.

This will enable you to keep a visual check on the egg's condition. Humidity is one of the most important factors for successful incubation. If the eggs are kept too wet, then fungal problems will almost certainly occur. If, on the other hand, the humidity is not high enough, then the eggs could dry out.

Keep the eggs slightly on the dry side and lightly spray them with tepid water on a daily basis. This daily routine means that the amount of water sprayed can be adjusted as and when you feel the eggs need it.

Reptile eggs absorb water as they develop, and can grow quite considerably, but too much water can be detrimental to the embryo.

The eggs need to be incubated at a temperature of around 30 degrees C (86 degrees F), although minor fluctuations do not seem to do that much harm.

The average incubation time is around 65 days but this can vary quite considerably, depending on exact temperatures and conditions.

SEX INFLUENCE

It would be remiss not to mention Temperature Sex Determination (TSD) as this is a well-observed phenomenon in Leopard Geckos, and quite a few other animals as well, including birds.

It has been noted that Leopard Gecko eggs incubated at the lower end of the tolerable incubation temperature, 28 degrees C (82 degrees F), will mostly result in hatchling females, while eggs incubated at the higher end of the tolerable incubation temperature, 32 degrees C (90 degrees F), will almost certainly result in males.

HATCHING

When freshly laid, the eggs should be white, soft and typically egg-shaped. They should measure anything from 20-30 mm (0.75-1.25 inches) in length, reaching at least half the length again by the time they hatch.

During the development of the eggs, it is quite natural for them to swell unevenly, and even to discolour slightly, while infertile or incorrectly maintained eggs will often collapse and/or blacken.

Sometimes, mould starts to develop on the eggs and, although not a good sign, it does not necessarily mean that the eggs are bad. It might just be caused by insufficient ventilation in the egg box.

If the mould is carefully cleaned off with a wet cotton bud, and extra ventilation provided, then sometimes the condition can be remedied.

If, during incubation, the eggs start to collapse, this might be due to insufficient humidity causing the eggs to dry out but, with a little bit of luck and if caught in time, regular spraying of the eggs can rectify the problem.

Immediately prior to hatching, small, faint, black lines can often be seen on the eggs. This is where the baby Leopard Gecko has started to cut open the egg with his egg tooth. The egg tooth is a tiny, forward-facing tooth on the upper jaw used specifically to open the egg; the tooth falls off soon after hatching.

Once the incision has been made, the Leopard Gecko is free to crawl out of the egg and make his own way in the world. Quite often, you will find a hole in the egg with just the tip of the lizard's nose sticking out, as some Leopard Geckos seem to delight in teasing an impatient observer

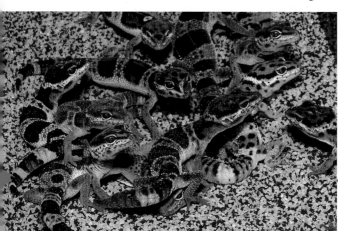

A gecko may take as long as 12 hours to break out of its egg.

Young geckos have a strong survival instinct, and may appear quite aggressive, but this is a temporary phase.

by adamantly refusing to leave the egg while being watched. If this is the case, then do not cause them any unnecessary stress; just leave them alone (preferably in the dark) and let them come out in their own time.

If, after about twelve hours, the lizard still has not made an appearance, then carefully tear the hole in the egg slightly wider. Only attempt this if you are reasonably certain that the lizard is definitely trying to hatch.

REARING

Once hatched, the baby Leopard Geckos can be transferred to a rearing container. This can either be a small vivarium, a plastic tank or even a large ice-cream tub, suitably ventilated, with either a heater mat underneath or the whole container placed in the vivarium with the adults. On no account should the babies be placed loose with the adults. Parental care does not enter into a Leopard Gecko's vocabulary and

the youngsters are more likely to be considered as a tasty snack rather than as mom and dad's pride and joy.

For at least the first few weeks of the Leopard Gecko's life, use kitchen towels (the tissue type) as a substrate. They are clean, cheap and unlikely to interfere with the lizard's first few attempts to catch his prey.

Leopard Geckos hatch with some of the umbilical cord still attached. This should be left alone, as it will dry up and fall off naturally within a few days.

Hatchling Leopard Geckos have, in common with most hatchling reptiles, a strong survival instinct.

They will frequently emit an audible hiss when handled and even strike at a nearby hand or finger. This attitude can be quite disconcerting for a novice keeper but do not worry. A hatchling Leopard Gecko is far too small to inflict any pain or injury and this behaviour will usually wear off within a few days.

6 The Gecko Varieties

The Leopard Gecko is usually the first choice for novice reptile-keepers because it is so easy to care for and to handle, and it has such a docile nature.

However, there is a huge range of different geckos available in pet shops, with a variety of appealing characteristics.

They all have slightly different husbandry requirements and traits, so included in this chapter are some details of the more commonly kept and easily available species.

The 800-plus species of gecko are split into four basic sub-families, with each member of a family sharing similar characteristics with other species in the same group.

Many of the diurnal (active during the daytime) geckos require ultraviolet (UV) lighting. This is not to enhance the aesthetic quality of the vivarium, but is actually an essential dietary requirement which, if ignored, will result in long-term deformity and disease. The UV radiation is required in order for the animal to synthesise vitamin D3, which is essential for the absorption of calcium from the lizard's diet.

THE FOUR SUB-FAMILIES

GEKKONINAE
(Typical geckos)
This is the largest group. They have the ability to vocalise, and may or may not have adhesive lamellae on their toes. The majority of geckos sold commercially come from this sub-family.

Examples of these would include:

- *Gekko Gecko*, also known as the Tokay Gecko
- Wonder Gecko
- House Geckos
- Turkish and Moorish Geckos
- Phelsumas or Day Geckos.

EUBLEPHARINE
(Eyelid geckos)
This is the only group that has movable eyelids; these lizards also have claws on their toes in place of the typical adhesive lamellae usually attributed to geckos.

An example of this sub-family would be the Leopard Gecko.

DIPLODACTYLINAE
(Double-fingered geckos)
This group is found only in Australasia and includes the largest species of gecko. They, too, can vocalise, and some species from this group give birth to live young instead of laying eggs.

SPHERODACTYLINAE
(Sphere-fingered geckos)
All within this group are small diurnal or crepuscular species (which means they are active in twilight), found in New World regions only. The smallest gecko species are found in this sub-family.

THE TOKAY GECKO
(Gekko Gecko)

ORIGIN
These large geckos are frequently imported for the pet trade from their countries of origin, which include North-eastern India, Bangladesh, Burma, Southern China, Malaysia, Indonesia, the Philippines and parts of the Indo-Australasian archipelago.

IDENTIFICATION
The Tokay Gecko is quite distinct and easily identifiable.

Growing quite large, up to 25 cm (10 inches) long, it possesses a bright grey/blue coloration, with distinctive paler blue and orange/red spots all over.

The colour varies in intensity with mood, temperature and hormonal changes, and can become quite drab-looking in cold or stressed animals.

These geckos have large, adhesive lamellae on their toes and, consequently, are excellent climbers.

They are an aggressive, noisy species that gained their name from the to-kay barking sound the males make when they call during mating or if they are being threatened.

When threatened, Tokay Geckos display an open-mouthed posture and will attempt to bite.

HABITAT
Primarily they were found in tropical rain forests. They have now adapted successfully to the modern world and frequently colonise human habitations.

Tokay Gecko: A species which tends to be quite noisy and aggressive.

TEMPERATURE

All pokilothermic animals need a varied temperature range within their environment so that they can choose where, and at what temperature, they need to be.

It is recommended that, for this species, you provide a daytime temperature of between 27 degrees C (80 degrees F) and 35 degrees C (95 degrees F) with a 'hot spot' under a heat lamp. At night the temperature in the vivarium should drop slightly to between about 22 degrees C (71 degrees F) and 25 degrees C (77 degrees F).

Heat can be provided in the forms discussed earlier.

HUMIDITY

The vivarium will need a light spraying with tepid water on a daily basis in order to maintain an average humidity of about 50 to 60 per cent.

LIGHTING

Requirements are identical to the requirement for the Leopard Gecko. These geckos are mainly nocturnal in habit, so extreme bright light will be for your benefit only.

In fact, it will probably encourage the animal to hide away. No ultraviolet light will be necessary.

DIET

These are voracious eaters and will require as varied a diet of invertebrates as you can provide. They will eat locusts, crickets, moths, mealworm, waxmoth larvae and even defrosted frozen small mice or pinkies.

It is prudent to dust the invertebrates with a vitamin and mineral supplement to help maintain the good health of your lizard.

BREEDING

The Tokay will lay several clutches of two eggs, which they stick to surfaces in the vivarium, usually in warm, dark, damp spots.

The eggs, once stuck to the wall, will be damaged unless extreme care is taken when moving them.

They may be better protected by having a small mesh cage placed over them. This will also contain the young when they hatch. The eggs require an incubation period of 100 to 182 days. The male will guard the eggs during this time.

After the black-and-white banded neonates hatch, watch over them carefully.

However, to prevent unwanted accidents, it is probably in the neonates' best interest to move them to another vivarium.

COMMENTS

If you wish to keep a gloriously-coloured, large gecko then this is one of the most vivid. Its major drawback is the difficulty in handling such an aggressive species, which is guaranteed to bite.

Herpetologists frequently keep them loose in heated reptile rooms with a small hide box in the top corner of the room, just to clear up any escaped food items from other lizard enclosures.

The need to catch or handle them is minimal and they thrive on the surplus food, so are considered by many to be a useful friend.

THE WONDER GECKO
(Teratoscincus scincus)

ORIGIN

These lovely little 'frog-eyed' lizards hail from a huge area extending from southern Russia, through south-western China, into central Asia and Iran.

THE GECKO VARIETIES

IDENTIFICATION

These little geckos grow to about 18 to 20 cm (7 to 8 inches) maximum.

They have a large head, with big round eyes. Their toes have a useful fringe-like edge to them to help them move through the substrate.

Distinctively, they have large fish-like scales on the body and tail, with smaller scales on their heads.

Their skin colour is pale to bright yellow, with black and dark brown flecks and stripes; they have some grey scales on their tail.

Their skin is very delicate, which aids respiration, but it tears very easily, so extra care has to be taken when handling them. This is a very attractive, docile species.

HABITAT

Their native habitat is sandy clay deserts and semi-desert areas. Possessing such fine, delicate skin in such harsh, hot habitats, is it any wonder how this species got its name?

To survive in such an environment, they dig burrows up to 80 cm (32 inches) deep, down into the damp layers beneath the

Wonder Gecko: This 'frog-eyed' gecko is docile in temperament but requires careful handling as it has delicate skin.

desert surface. This natural behaviour should be taken into account when setting up their vivarium, and deep layers of substrate should be provided.

TEMPERATURE

Obviously, a desert species will require a fairly hot vivarium but do not forget to incorporate a temperature range in order to give the animal choice.

A daytime temperature of about 32 degrees C (90 degrees F) to 35 degrees C (95 degrees F), with a higher local surface temperature of about 40 degrees C (104 degrees F) in one area, should suffice.

The night-time temperature drop should be approximately 10 degrees C (50 degrees F) to about 20 to 22 degrees C (68 to 72 degrees F). Heating can be provided by heat lamps, light bulbs, heater pads, or hot rocks.

HUMIDITY

Since they are a desert-dwelling species, a low level of humidity should be provided, but they do require access to plenty of clean drinking water.

LIGHTING

The Wonder Gecko is mainly crepuscular, with some nocturnal habits. It is a burrowing species that would not stand much chance of survival in the desert if it appeared during the extreme heat of the daytime.

You will not need to provide ultraviolet light. The light from the heat lamps should be sufficient.

DIET

This little gecko will readily eat a variety of invertebrates of an appropriate size, such as crickets or locust hoppers. Dust the insect food with a vitamin and mineral supplement to ensure that all dietary requirements are being met.

BREEDING

In order to breed, Wonder Geckos require a brief (two- to three-week) winter rest period, at a slightly lowered temperature.

Be warned, gravid females become very aggressive towards the more docile males who are reluctant to defend themselves. This can prove fatal, so it is recommended that the males are removed while the females are pregnant.

The females produce four clutches of two eggs. A surprisingly low humidity of about 40 to 65 per cent is needed to hatch their eggs. Incubation takes approximately 72 to 93 days when incubated at a temperature of 28 degrees C to 32 degrees C (82.5 to 90 degrees F).

COMMENTS

These beautiful little lizards tame down very readily and are usually no problem to handle, showing very little aggression. Care should be taken, however, since the skin is very delicate, and these animals have a tendency to lose their tails.

This species should pose little problem to keep in captivity, provided that the correct husbandry procedure is maintained.

HOUSE GECKOS
(*Hemidactylus* spp.)

Large numbers of these House Geckos are caught, en masse, in the wild, and regularly imported for the pet trade, ultimately ending up all mixed together.

There are a number of different species, all in the family *Hemidactylus*, that fall into this category.

They include *Hemidactylus flaviviridis*, the East African House Gecko, the *Hemidactylus frenatus* or, the Indian House Gecko, frequently called the Chitchat Gecko, and also the Turkish Gecko *Hemidactylus turicus*. Although they have some differences, they share roughly the same husbandry requirements.

ORIGIN

Originally found only in South East Asia, they have spread to all tropical continents. The Turkish is found on the coasts of the Mediterranean and as far east as Pakistan.

IDENTIFICATION

A small, nondescript gecko growing, on average, to about 12 cm (5 inches) in length, with some, such as *flaviviridis*, growing to 15 cm (6 inches). The *Frenatus* sp. is slender and agile with a narrow tail.

The body is covered in small, granular scales while the tail has cone-shaped scales. Their background colour is a yellowish-brown and they occasionally have two dark longitudinal stripes on their upper flanks.

Flaviviridis has a background colour varying from light grey to yellowish-brown with a darker marbling pattern on its back.

These geckos have adhesive lamellae on their toe pads and are very fast-moving.

Turkish Geckos have a base colour of pale yellow, or sand, and can even be pinkish-grey with tubercular scales and a surface-covering of brown and white spotting.

HABITAT

Their natural habitat is woods, thickets and cultivated land, but they have readily colonised human settlements, ruins, stone walls, etc.

The vivarium should try to imitate this by providing artificial plants, bark caves and branches for cover.

TEMPERATURE

A gradient should be provided throughout the vivarium within the range 20 degrees C (68 degrees F) to 30 degrees C (86 degrees F) by day, with a hot basking spot somewhere in the vivarium just over 30 degrees C. They will need a slight drop at night to between 20 degrees C (68 degrees F) and 25 degrees C (77 degrees F).

HUMIDITY

A reasonably high humidity of about 70 per cent to 90 per cent can be maintained in the vivarium by daily spraying with tepid water.

Using a substrate that retains moisture, such as peat or sphagnum moss, should assist in maintaining this required level of humidity.

LIGHTING

House Geckos are generally crepuscular or nocturnal, so do not require ultraviolet light. They may benefit from a basking lamp placed above a flat rock.

Care should be taken to cover any exposed bulbs or heating elements, since these geckos have adhesive lamellae on their feet and could inadvertently burn themselves.

DIET

A variety of insects dusted with a vitamin/mineral supplement should be provided. Water will frequently be drunk from the sprayed droplets that are retained on the tank decor.

An occasional vitamin and sugar lick may be provided by mixing a little honey with vitamin powder until a fairly solid consistency is obtained, then putting the mixture into a bottle cap and attaching it to the wall of the vivarium.

The lizards will eagerly lick this addition to their diet, thus ensuring a good intake of vitamins and minerals.

HANDLING

These are very fast-moving, small, delicate lizards, with lamellated feet allowing them to climb vertical surfaces.

Always handle them with care and as infrequently as possible. And remember, once loose they are almost impossible to retrieve.

BREEDING

Some of these geckos will require a six- to eight-week winter rest period at a reduced temperature prior to breeding.

The females usually lay about three to five clutches of two eggs a year; they do not bury them but leave them where they believe they are most likely to hatch, which tends to be on the walls and decor of the tank.

It is best to remove them if you can and incubate them separately. *Frenatus* will require a 47- to 55-day incubation at a temperature of approximately 32 degrees C (90 degrees F).

Flaviviridis on the other hand, need an incubation of 60 days at approximately 26 degrees C (79 degrees F) and 60 per cent humidity.

The Turkish have an incubation period of 41 to 50 days at 28 degrees C (82.5 degrees F) to 31

degrees C (88 degrees F) and a humidity of 60 per cent plus.

COMMENTS

These are very pretty geckos and very entertaining to watch. They breed fairly easily, and are a relatively easy lizard to maintain.

Caution should be taken when handling, to protect their delicate skin and to prevent escapes.

BIBRONS GECKO
(Pachydactylus bibrini)

ORIGIN

These geckos hail from Africa, south of the Sahara.

IDENTIFICATION

Bibrons grow up to approximately 18 to 20 cm (7 to 8 inches) in length.

This is a chubby-looking little lizard with a wide head; the large eyes have vertical pupils typical of a nocturnal species.

They have fat-looking toes because of the well-developed adhesive pads that aid climbing. This has given the *Pachydactylus* family the nickname 'thick-toed geckos'.

The skin's background colour is pale and the very tubercular scales are interspersed with numerous

Bibrons Gecko: Easy to keep and blessed with a long life span.

white and brown spots. In some, the darker spots join up into recognisable bands of colour.

HABITAT

The Bibrons' natural habitat includes numerous damp areas, so this should be considered when designing their vivarium. Sphagnum moss, or peat, as a suitable substrate would be ideal, as well as a generously planted area.

TEMPERATURE

Their origin and preferred habitat will give clues as to their required temperature: hot and humid.

Provide a good temperature gradient throughout the vivarium, with 'hot spots' and cooler areas in order for the animal to self-regulate its temperature.

A daytime temperature within the tank of between 25 degrees C (77 degrees F) and 32 degrees C (90 degrees F), with one area under a 'hot spot' for intense basking, is required.

A slight drop in temperature at night can then be achieved by turning off this basking lamp.

LIGHTING

Since they are, for the most part, crepuscular, they do not require ultraviolet light.

HUMIDITY

To maintain a high humidity, the vivarium should be well planted with non-poisonous live plants in peat or moss, or artificial plants can be used. Daily spraying with tepid water will be necessary.

The lizard is likely to drink from

water droplets on the plants, but if a drinking water bowl is placed near a heat source (e.g. heater mat), the natural evaporation of this will aid humidity levels.

DIET
An insectivorous lizard, just like the other geckos, will require a varied supply of invertebrates, from crickets to moth larvae, dusted with a vitamin and mineral food supplement to help maintain good health.

COMMENTS
These very pretty, agile and social lizards make excellent pets. They are enthusiastic feeders and fun to watch. They have a long life span and can be very rewarding.

Because of their ability to climb any surface and move very quickly, care must be taken if they are to be handled to ensure that they do not escape.

MOORISH GECKOS OR WALL GECKOS
(Tarentola mauritanica)

ORIGIN
These geckos originate from the Iberian Peninsula, the Balearic and Pityusen islands, Southern France, Corsica, Sardinia, the Italian coast, the North Adriatic, Crete and North Africa.

IDENTIFICATION
The Moorish Gecko grows to 16 cm (6.5 inches) in length; its head, body and ringed tail appear to have a distinctly flattened appearance.

It has plump-looking 'sticky feet' with adhesive lamellae. Its body is covered in a combination of small, angular and larger, keeled scales.

The body's base colour is a creamy-white to yellowish-brown, and even dark brown to black, with darker bands in juveniles that fade with age.

The colour varies depending on temperature, mood and hormone levels.

HABITAT
Moorish Geckos are frequently found inhabiting buildings, ruins, bridges, stone walls, rocky outcrops and piles of stone.

TEMPERATURE
A temperature gradient should be provided from 29 degrees C (84 degrees F) to 34 degrees C (93.2 degrees F), with a hot spot of about 35 degrees C (95 degrees F) from a heat lamp for basking.

Heating can be provided by heat

mats, protected ceramic heat lamps, light bulbs or hot rocks.

HUMIDITY

A tall vivarium should be provided with appropriate decor such as a false brick or wall background, piles of rocks or stone, and even bark caves.

The humidity levels in such a vivarium would consequently be quite low, but a shallow drinking bowl is essential, filled daily with fresh water.

LIGHTING

For the most part, the Moorish Gecko is crepuscular, active at dawn and dusk, and nocturnal, busy catching insects drawn to human habitation lights.

They occasionally are seen basking on rocks as the sun rises, so it is best to provide a hot basking spot with a light bulb in the vivarium.

DIET

A variety of invertebrates should be provided, well dusted with vitamin and mineral supplements to prevent the onset of dietary disorders.

COMMENTS

This very agile gecko is very entertaining in an appropriate vivarium and can be kept in pairs. Adult males can be very territorial so only one adult male per vivarium is recommended. They take about four to five years to reach sexual maturity.

Sexing is very difficult since there is little sexual dimorphism.

If you keep a number of young specimens together, usually the first indication that there is more than one adult male in the vivarium is when a fight breaks out. If you have a good breeder, or local supplier, they will usually exchange surplus males either for younger specimens or for known females.

This is also a long-lived species and comes highly recommended as a suitable beginner's gecko. Like the House Geckos, the speed and agility of this little one can make handling difficult, and escapees are difficult to retrieve.

MADAGASCAR DAY GECKOS
(Phelsuma spp.)

There are a number of *Phelsuma* species. Fortunately all have similar husbandry requirements. They can, however, be very territorial, so a large vivarium with plenty of hiding places and plenty of height is recommended.

THE GECKO VARIETIES

Some examples of these Day Geckos include *Phelsuma madagascariensis grandis*, the Giant Day Gecko, *Phelsuma laticauda*, the Gold Dust Day Gecko, *Phelsuma quadriocellata*, the Peacock Day Gecko, and *Phelsuma standingi*, the Banded Day Gecko.

ORIGIN
The family *phelsuma* includes a rather unique group of geckos found on the island of Madagascar.

They are diurnal lizards, active during daylight hours, hence the name. Because this makes them more vulnerable to predators, they have evolved a range of vivid skin coloration to camouflage them in the tropical forests and plantations. It is this coloration that makes them so attractive as pets.

Since they are a protected species it is usually only captive-bred specimens that are available to the pet trade.

IDENTIFICATION
These stunningly attractive geckos are easily recognisable because of their vivid green to gold colours. There are a couple of species of a duller olive to grey-brown hue, but these are rarely available as pets.

The green coloration is usually marked with bright red or blue flashes, which vary from species to species.

Day Gecko: Stunning to look at, these geckos need plenty of branches for climbing.

Being arboreal, they have lamellae on their toes which can make catching them within the vivarium difficult.

Like all diurnal lizards, they have round pupils. The males have distinctly broader heads, and females have calcium deposits on each side of their neck.

This is a fairly large gecko. The largest species, the Giant Madagascar Day Gecko, grows up to 28 cm (11 inches) in length.

HABITAT

Their natural habitat is tropical forests and plantations, but they are occasionally found following human habitations. The spacious, tall, vivarium should, therefore, be well planted, with plenty of climbing branches, and have a suitable substrate to help maintain humidity levels, such as peat or sphagnum moss.

The geckos will require some flat areas near basking lamps and plenty of hiding places, such as cork bark tubes, attached to the wall of the vivarium, since *phelsumas* rarely come down to the substrate.

When decorating the vivarium, always remember to sterilise branches and ensure that any potentially poisonous mosses or lichens are removed.

TEMPERATURE

A gradient should be provided with cooler and warmer areas and 'hot spots' within the vivarium. Daytime temperatures should be around the 25 degree C (77 degrees F) to 30 degree C (86 degrees F) range; this should be reduced by around 10 degrees at night to about 20 degrees C (68 degrees F) to 22 degrees C (72 degrees F).

HUMIDITY

In order to reproduce their natural habitat as closely as possible, humidity levels should be around 60 per cent to 80 per cent. This can be achieved by using suitable moisture-retaining substrate, and regular daily spraying of the vegetation with tepid water.

Since these geckos are reluctant to come down to the substrate level of the vivarium, small drinking water vessels should be attached to the walls of the vivarium at suitable points. The geckos may prefer to drink water droplets from the vegetation, but it is always good to give them the option.

LIGHTING

Since these are diurnal lizards, it is essential that, in conjunction with the basking lamps placed in the large vivarium, you should also provide ultraviolet fluorescent lighting.

These are commercially available and easy to use. The lifespan of the ultraviolet rays produced by these tubes is usually only 12 to 18 months so, even though they may be producing light after this period of time, insufficient ultraviolet rays will be generated.

The penetration of the rays is also limited to approximately 18 inches (45 cms) so position them accordingly in the vivarium.

When using high watt basking or heat lamps for geckos possessing lamellated feet, enclose the bulb in a mesh cage to prevent the geckos climbing on to the hot surface and severely burning their feet.

DIET
The *phelsumas* will eat a variety of invertebrates, including crickets, locust hoppers, moths, and waxmoth larvae. They will occasionally eat small, diced pieces of soft, sweet fruit.

A vitamin/mineral supplement should be used to dust the food items. They will require additional calcium in their diet, especially prior to egg laying.

The females have pouches, in which they store calcium, on either side of their neck. They are also partial to honey, so the best way to introduce additional calcium or vitamins into the diet is to make an occasional honey lick.

HANDLING
The *phelsumas* are a more substantial gecko than the House Geckos, for example, and, although they are also agile and have adhesive lamellae on their feet, they are easier to handle, once caught.

They are less likely to bite than the Tokay. For the most part, they should be observed rather than handled, since excessive handling of any *phelsuma* will stress the animal unnecessarily.

BREEDING
The females will lay clutches of one or two eggs several times during the breeding season, in secluded corners of the vivarium or at the base of plants.

An incubation period of approximately 65 days at a temperature of about 28 degrees C (82.5 degrees F) and average humidity of 70 per cent is required.

7 *Health Care And Ailments*

If you purchase a captive-bred gecko and keep it in the conditions outlined in this book, then the chances of encountering any health problems are quite remote.

Leopard Geckos are, generally, extremely hardy little creatures, with the vast majority of ailments being the direct result of bad husbandry. Fouled water and contact with stale faecal matter are responsible for most diseases in the vivarium. So, the message is simple. Keep the vivarium clean.

Wild-caught geckos can be somewhat more problematical. Even the hardiest of animals is unlikely to escape unscathed from the barbaric conditions that the poor wretches have to endure during shipping.

Leopard Geckos are hardy creatures, and most will suffer few health problems.

Sometimes small patches of skin remain on the body after shedding.

COMMON AILMENTS

Most of the problems that you are likely to encounter are, if recognised early enough, easily rectified; but it is the delay between diagnosis and treatment that is critical.

This chapter describes some of the more common ailments and injuries, together with suggested remedies.

Please remember that, although we would fully endorse treating the animals yourself wherever possible, if you have the slightest doubt over your diagnosis, or the effectiveness of any remedy attempted, then seek professional assistance urgently.

The cost of a vet when weighed against the wellbeing and cost of a replacement lizard quickly balances out.

CUTS AND GRAZES

Virtually all minor wounds, whether they be from squabbling, from sharp objects or even through rough handling, can be treated easily by applying any of the iodine-based solutions available from most good pet shops or vets. It is a good idea to keep one of these medicines on hand as rapid treatment goes a long way to preventing infection.

Should infection set in, which is easily recognised by either a swelling or a mucous discharge, or both, at the site of the wound, then professional treatment with antibiotics must be sought.

Some of the larger cuts, particularly ones that keep reopening instead of healing, will probably need to have stitches put in by the vet.

SKIN SHEDDING

Occasionally, during the course of shedding skin (Ecdysis), small patches of skin remain on the body. If discovered early, and before they have dried out, they will pull off quite easily. If they have dried out, then it will sometimes be necessary to bathe the area in tepid water to soften the skin before it can be removed.

It is generally not essential to remove these patches of skin from the body as, apart from giving a slightly leper-like appearance to the lizard, they seldom cause any harm. However, it would be wise to ensure that such patches come off with the next shed, otherwise so many layers are built up that they will be almost impossible to remove.

Where it is essential to remove stubborn patches of skin is around the toes. Occasionally during shedding, the skin around the gecko's feet remains behind, often resembling a 'glove', though sometimes it might be just a 'finger' or two. If this skin is not removed then, as it dries, it can restrict the blood flow to the digits, usually to the extent that they will actually shrivel up and fall off.

Again, this can be remedied, if noticed early enough, by just gently pulling the skin off. If, however, the skin has had a chance to dry and become stubborn, then any over-zealous pulling at it can actually do as much damage as the loss of circulation itself.

The best method to remove the

The easiest way to remove stubborn patches of skin is to place the gecko in a bowl of shallow, tepid water.

skin is to stand the gecko in a shallow bowl of tepid water for about fifteen minutes to soften the skin.

If this process does not work the first time, then repeat it. Eventually the offending skin will become soft enough to almost fall off by itself.

TAIL SHEDDING

As mentioned earlier in this book, Leopard and most other geckos, have the ability to shed their tails (autotomy) under times of threat. Unfortunately, this can also occur through rough handling or even during heated disagreements amongst themselves.

Although such an event appears quite dramatic to the observer, there is seldom any lasting effect on the animal.

However, the site at which the Leopard Gecko actually drops its tail is self-sealing and, therefore, should not require any treatment, but it would do no harm to keep a visual check on the area until the tail has started to regenerate.

It is interesting to note that, occasionally, geckos that have sustained injury to the base of the tail, but without actually dropping it, have been known to regenerate a second, fork-like tail.

MOUTH ROT

Mouth rot (stomatitis) is a rather unpleasant condition, easily recognised in the early stages as a swelling in the mouth, often so bad that it stops the animal closing its mouth.

The other main symptoms include bleeding from the gums, cheese-like deposits around the infected area and loss of appetite.

There are several causes of mouth rot. The most common is as a result of an injury to the mouth, or from an infected, unshed tooth. Lizards shed and regenerate new teeth throughout their lives.

Mouth rot is really a secondary disease, afflicting animals whose resistance has been lowered either by stress (through bad husbandry), from a vitamin deficiency, or even by a parasite infestation.

If the condition is caught in the early stages, treatment is relatively simple. Keep the affected area clean and remove any build-up of necrotic, mucky tissue, using a cotton bud and a suitable antiseptic solution. If you are unsure what to use, then get your local pet shop or vet to advise you.

In chronic cases, a trip to the vet

Turnip Tailed Gecko.

for treatment with antibiotics is vital as, if left unchecked, mouth rot will prove fatal and can spread to other occupants in the vivarium.

It is important to remember that any treatment will be futile unless the underlying cause of the animal's lowered resistance to disease is rectified.

I would recommend an increase in the amount of vitamin supplement offered, and a thorough review of the conditions within the vivarium, from correct temperature through to hygiene.

PARASITES

A parasite, by definition, is any animal that lives either in, or on its host's body without contributing in any way to the host's welfare.

Most wild reptiles carry a small population of parasites which, on a healthy animal, pose no real threat. However, within the confines of a vivarium, or on a weakened or stressed individual, parasite populations can explode to lethal proportions.

Identification and eradication of most of the commonly encountered parasites is normally a reasonably straightforward affair and quite easy for even the most novice of keepers to treat but, occasionally, particularly tenacious or resistant parasites rear their ugly heads and defy the broader-spectrum remedies.

In these cases veterinary assistance will be required to identify the specific organism responsible and to recommend the specific treatment to eradicate it.

EXTERNAL PARASITES (ECTOPARASITES)

There are only two forms of external parasite that need concern the gecko-keeper, ticks and mites. Ticks and mites are small, eight-legged invertebrates related to the spider.

They have sharp, piercing mouthparts that are used to puncture the skin in order to reach the blood vessels underneath. This behaviour can make them a vector for disease between one animal and another.

A gecko's behaviour can indicate if it is infested with mites or ticks. The main clues are prolonged periods of bathing (often leaving the drowned bodies of the parasites behind in the water container), shedding difficulties, or, more obviously, constant rubbing or scratching against objects in the vivarium.

TICKS

Ticks, the larger of the two ectoparasites, are readily visible to the naked eye. They look a bit like an enlarged scale with legs but, as they gorge themselves on the unfortunate host's blood, their abdomen swells up noticeably.

One way to kill ticks is to cover their abdomens with a blob of petroleum jelly. This fouls their breathing apparatus, forcing them to let go of their host.

A quicker way of eradicating ticks is to remove them manually. This can be done either with a pair of tweezers or with small forceps. By gently twisting, back and forth, the body of the tick, it

White Striped Gecko.

High Yellow Leopard Gecko.

can eventually be persuaded to release its hold on the host.

Never just pull the tick off the animal. If you do that, the chances are that the tick's head will snap off and be left to decay in the host's skin, probably causing an infection.

Due to the relatively complicated lifecycle of the tick, re-infestation of a 'clean' animal is unlikely to occur in a captive environment.

MITES

Mites, the more commonly encountered ectoparasite, are considerably smaller than ticks and a lot harder to spot. They resemble dark, pinhead-size dots moving over the gecko's body, tending to congregate in areas of soft tissue such as around the eyes, ears, the vent and the lizard's equivalent to armpits.

Several errant mites can sometimes be noticed on your hands immediately after handling the animal, thus demonstrating the ease in which infestation can spread from one vivarium to another unless strict hygiene regimes are employed.

There are several sprays now available on the market designed to eradicate mites, but they can be expensive and not particularly effective.

A favoured remedy is to bathe all the occupants of the vivarium in tepid water to get rid of as many mites as possible, and meticulously to disinfect the vivarium and all its contents.

This will kill most of the mites in the vivarium but is unlikely to damage the near-indestructible eggs that the mites lay in minute cracks or crevices.

Use one of the insecticide strips found in vets' surgeries and chemist shops, but care must be taken not to overdose the very animal you are trying to treat.

The best way to do this is to cut off a 30 mm (1.2 inch) square section of the insecticide-impregnated strip, more for vivaria large enough to hold groups of four or more lizards, and place it in a well-ventilated plastic tub in the vivarium.

By placing the strip in the tub, you prevent the geckos having direct access to it and possibly poisoning themselves.

Painted Ground Gecko.

Leaving the strip in the vivarium for around five days should kill all remaining adult and recently-hatched mites.

The strip should then be taken out of the vivarium for another five days. This will give the geckos a break from the effects of the strip.

By the time the five days are up, all the remaining mite eggs should have hatched and the strip will then kill all the immature mites before they have a chance to lay their own eggs. If, after this, the mites are still present, the process can be repeated.

There have been reports that some strains of mite are developing a resistance to the insecticides used in these strips so, if after several applications there is

no improvement, go to the vet. There are injections available that render the reptile's blood toxic to parasites but, generally, these can be expensive.

INTERNAL PARASITES

Various internal parasites can be found in reptiles. Some never make their presence felt in a healthy animal but, occasionally, and usually due to external factors such as bad husbandry or stress, these parasites can flare up to problematic proportions which, if left untreated, can have disastrous results.

The three most commonly encountered endoparasites are roundworms (nematodes), tapeworms (cestodes) and flukes (trematodes).

Symptoms of an internal parasite infestation vary depending on the organism responsible and can range from unusual, or even blood-streaked, faeces to respiratory problems such as laboured breathing or, possibly, a swollen abdomen. Sometimes adult worms, or more usually their eggs, are passed along with the faeces.

The main symptom, common to all of these parasites, is an overall loss in general condition. An infected lizard will be lethargic with half-closed, often sunken eyes, dramatic weight loss particularly noticeable around the hip area, and eventually a complete loss of appetite.

Treatment with a general wormer from your local vet will normally remedy the problem quite quickly. This is usually a liquid that you can administer yourself with the aid of a dropper, by simply holding open the lizard's mouth, using something fairly rigid but not hard enough to damage the mouth. Drop the liquid into the back of the lizard's throat, following the dosage instructions carefully.

This treatment will have to be repeated about a fortnight later to kill all the newly hatched parasites, as the eggs are impervious to the treatment.

Do not use the proprietary brands of wormer used for cats and dogs, as some of these contain agents that are as toxic to reptiles as they are to parasites.

If after two to three weeks of this course of treatment there is no visible improvement in the patient's condition, then a further trip to the vet will be necessary for a more exact identification and treatment of the organism

Flying Gecko: With good care and management, your gecko should remain fit and well for the duration of his life.

involved. This will usually involve analysis of a fresh faecal sample for the parasite's eggs.

Once the parasites have been eradicated from the animal, then re-infestation in captivity is unlikely. This is due to the lifecycle of most of these parasites, which generally require at least one intermediary host to be able to develop into adults. However, some of the parasites can gain access to the host by being ingested with food or water contaminated by faeces – yet another reason why strict hygiene is a must.

NON-FEEDING

Loss of appetite in a gecko can be due to a number of reasons. Any of the ailments already listed can put a lizard off its food.

A recently purchased, or just moved, lizard will often fast while it adjusts to its new environment, though this should really only be for a matter of days.

Quite frequently, a gecko will refuse food for a few days prior to shedding its skin. A temporary fast does a gecko no harm at all but if, after a week, the animal is still showing no interest in food, then it is indicative of a problem.

If the animal seems to be in general good health and not displaying any of the signs or symptoms already discussed, then the most likely cause is temperature.

If the temperature in your vivarium is too low, then the lizard's digestive system slows down, or even stops. If the lizard feels that he cannot digest food, then obviously he is unlikely to eat it in the first place.

Increasing the temperature in the vivarium can easily rectify this problem. This should be done with some urgency as any food remaining in the stomach without being digested will rot and poison the animal.

Another possible cause for loss of appetite in geckos is stress. If a lizard feels threatened in any way, either by another lizard or even by too frequent rough handling, then this will put him off his food.

If you suspect either of these reasons, then separate the animal or leave him alone for several days and then offer him food.

If this works, then build your gecko up with extra food before putting him back in his vivarium with a more considerate handling regime.

COLDS

Even reptiles can suffer from their own version of this rather infuriating malady. A Leopard Gecko can develop a cold if it has been 'chilled' or even just kept at slightly too low a temperature for too long.

The symptoms are easy to spot and include discharge from the nostrils, excessive mucus in the mouth and laboured breathing (panting), sometimes with an audible rattling sound.

If caught early, simply raising the temperature a couple of degrees above optimum will cure it. If it has really taken hold, then a short course of antibiotics from the vet will be needed.